The Magic of Zero

The Magic of Zero

*The Art of Finding Happiness
in the Land of Having*

Christina Florence, CHt

Edited by Elyse Barkin

Acknowledgements

I would like to thank my wonderful husband Walter for his unwavering support in the years it took me to write this book.

I'd like to also thank my mother and father and my five fabulous sisters for never giving up on me, even though I definitely tried their patience on many occasions.

Also a huge thanks to my partners on this project, Gary and Elyse. Without you, this would still be a stack of paper gathering dust on my desk.

Finally I am deeply indebted to all of my clients who have taught me so very much. You have all enriched me with your own stories of strength and will power and the magic of zero.

For Victoria

The important thing is not to stop questioning. Curiosity has its own reason for existing. One cannot help but be in awe when he contemplates the mysteries of eternity, of life, of the marvelous structure of reality. It is enough if one tries merely to comprehend a little of this mystery every day. Never lose a holy curiosity.

– Albert Einstein

Contents

Introduction

It has taken me a very long time to write this book, years in fact. I have always been fascinated by zero. I saw zeros in everything; in the clouds, in the bubbles in the dish soap, in seashells, and while I was driving. In fact one day I was driving on the highway and glanced at an upcoming mile marker which oddly enough had only zeros on it. I was going nowhere! I pondered this for a long time. Was I really going nowhere or was the Universe beseeching me to pay attention.

My constant musings about the nature of zero took shape as the foundation for this book. However, this foundation didn't often appear to be standing on any substantial ground. In fact it was so shaky that at times I believed my earlier question about whether I was indeed going nowhere was about to be confirmed.

The truth is after I put my initial thoughts on paper, I didn't write another thing for three years. I sat at my desk and stared at the stacks of papers and bills that were accumulating almost as fast as the dust was settling on my laptop.

During this time I came to understand that Zero itself is a place of beginning, whereas *The Magic of Zero* is the end result, abundance happiness and fulfillment. I told myself that someday I must finish this book. I fully intended to finish this book. When I could stand the inertia no longer I asked for help. Help came that very day in the form of my talented editor, Elyse Barkin and the serious work began.

This book will provide all the tools you need to help you transform your life into one of success, happiness and abundance. How did these tools transform my life? I will share my journey of transformation.

While it has taken me many years to journey through *The Magic of Zero* it is my intention in this book to shorten the amount of time it will take *you* to get there.

Don't compromise yourself. It's all you've got.
— Janis Joplin

My Story

I've always wondered why there were so many more "have nots" in the world than there were "haves." Everywhere I looked there were people with brains and an abundance of talent who seemed sadly to be sidelined when it came to the game of success and happiness. Unfortunately, I had to include myself in that category. I was a struggling dancer in New York City. I never had enough money to pay my rent, though I sometimes worked as many as three jobs. I was so depressed I could hardly make it to dance class, much less to an audition. So I began, what turned out to be, a twenty year study to figure out what was so different about me from those other people who seemed to be so effortlessly happy and successful. What was I missing? But, before we continue, let's flash back to the eighties for a few moments.

I moved to New York City fresh out of college, with a song on my lips and a dream in my heart, as the phrase goes. I was going to be famous. I'd be the toast of the town, the ballerina with both a movie contract and a recording contract. I'd have my own show. People in the remotest areas of the globe, on the smallest island would recognize me. I'd have recognition factor equivalent to that of Julia Roberts (or whoever was big at that time) in the Ballet world. I'd be Madonna before Madonna got the job. But, as it turned out, I was none of those things. New York would be the training ground for what would be my life's calling, as yet still quite a ways down the road. I lived in the city for twelve years with only a few brief but shining moments of notoriety. My fifteen minutes of fame was actually only about eight to ten minutes.

So there I was, going nowhere fast.

I was a fairly good dancer but I was terrified to audition. At 35, I was considered old in the dance world. Finally a knee injury forced me off my feet; I left New York and a failing relationship and headed home to heal. Of course I was going straight to Hollywood after that to become a famous actress. There my talents would definitely attract "I'd like to thank the Academy" acclaim. I just needed a little cash first and then I would surely be on my way. Just a short stay, in order to regroup, *you know*. Before long I had a job in a restaurant which ultimately ended, three years later, in my owning a restaurant. (Goodbye Hollywood, exit stage left.)

At the time, I had a partner with a dream. It was a good dream. But it was his dream. His dream to open a restaurant, and I got sucked in. I will spare you the gruesome details of what happens when you follow someone else's dream. But suffice to say I was left with all the debt, and then some, when it was all over four years later.

My restaurant experience took me backwards and forwards. Now I know that sometimes we have to go backward in order to move forward with self-assurance. Ultimately, I ended up $150,000 in debt and nowhere to go. Literally. And no real way to make the money I needed to get out of debt. My partner was nowhere to be found. The sad state of my circumstances forced to me move in with my father and take a job in a call center (two of the most humiliating experiences of my entire life). Well, there I was, certainly at Zero or so I thought.

Fear of failure had been my constant companion for years, inconveniently underfoot as I embarked on any new endeavor. I had been slowly slogging through the whining, the complaining, the big sighs, the tears, the laundry list of 1000 reasons why I couldn't, shouldn't, wouldn't until I finally reached the bottom. So, in what a friend of mine so aptly calls "a blinding glimpse of the obvious" I decided to sell my enormously unsuccessful restaurant and move on.

That year was a shock to my system. I had to file bankruptcy. Oh yes, now that I think of it, there were *three* humiliating experiences. And, I also had to eat a lot of crow. (Crow, eaten on good china with a nice little glass of claret can actually be quite tasty.) I ate quite a lot of it during those days. I was totally miserable. My partner had left me and I was in huge financial debt. I was living with my Dad and I felt like a baby. The feeling of loss was overwhelming.

Then, interestingly enough, that is the year things started to change for me. I started to look within and ask for help. I asked for help each day. I learned that in each of us there is a well of knowledge, a deep place of understanding. It is in this place that we find our own magic. I asked for this knowledge to be made accessible so I could act upon it. And then I did what I call "waiting for instructions." I asked to be shown my path. I asked to be taken care of.

I had the sense that I did not know where I was going and that I might never know. I would drive to the job at the call center, (Ugh! How I hated that job), and wonder how my life had come to this. But a little voice in my head kept saying "Something will change soon." I just had to wait.

Wait for instructions. As medical intuitive Carolyn Myss says in her book, *Why People Don't Heal and How They Can*, "Waiting allows the Divine to awaken the part of your spirit that contains the essence of what you are capable of contributing to others as well as yourself." This was hard. Anyone who knows me would tell you that waiting is just not my thing.

When you are forced to Zero it is because you have nowhere else to go. It is sometimes necessary for you to lose everything in order to get to Zero (but not essential). In my case I was just too stubborn to realize that I needed to change.

Since I was unwilling to initiate change on my own, the Powers That Be just stepped in and changed things for me. And sure enough, one day out of the blue a remarkable thing happened. I got fired from my job! So, there I was sitting out in the parking lot wondering what on earth I had done to deserve this, when my cell phone rang. It was a friend of mine who ran a metaphysical store telling me that he needed help and did I want a job! From that point on miraculous things started to happen to me. The knowledge I needed to change my life started coming to me from everywhere. Books would literally jump off the shelf at me at the bookstore. It seemed as though people were lining up to offer exactly the advice I was seeking.

And here's what I learned.

It takes 90 days to change a thought.

The most difficult obstacle to overcome is your "stuck-ness." When I say stuck I mean stuck. This means that no matter what you try there is a part of you that won't let go. Sometimes you just need to honor your stuck-ness. Don't push against it and don't try to change anything. Instead just ask for what you want and let the universe figure out the timing. Ask for help from whatever source you connect to and then just wait. Wait for instructions.

Waiting, as you know, is not something we twenty first century folk do well these days. We all succumb to the lure of instant gratification. Ours is a fast food world. Even one hour photo turned out to be too long so now we have digital. We want everything immediately. Just think, March 10, 1886, the telephone is invented. This, in the grand scheme of things, is not all that long ago. Before that we had nothing but letters that could take months to receive. Visiting someone 100 miles away was not the norm. So, waiting up to 90 days to change your thought process is work. It requires diligence and consistency. If work scares you and you don't think you can wait 90 days then you may end up remaining stuck. Consider this, say you wanted to have a baby... would your conversation with your doctor go something like this; "You know, I thought I had nine months penciled in for the birth process but as it turns out I only have three. Can you work with me on this?" I don't think so. In this case the nine months is not negotiable.

Change takes time for a good reason. Birthing a new you should not be a hurried process. You need to know who you really are and ease into it and get used to being a different person. Think of how long it took you to create all these negative thoughts in the first place. The problem is that we are impatient and want to see results, *now*. That's when you have to keep pushing. It is those last few steps up the mountain that are so difficult, yet so crucial. Perhaps the main reason we resist the process of becoming our authentic selves is that we intuitively know the price we may have to pay. As author Gregg Levoy says in his book, *Callings*, "We may have to give up something. Be it a lifestyle, anger at someone, a belief, precious time or just the pleasures of cynicism."

With the worst of my financial nightmares behind me and with a little (or a lot) of help from my friends, I took the next step.

I decided to become a Life Coach.

So, you ask, what did I know about being a Life Coach? Not one thing! I knew I wanted to be able to help people in a way that I didn't seem to be able to help myself. I asked the universe to send me the means with which to embark on my new career. Soon the means arrived in the form of a coaching course which then resulted in two certificates quite suitable for framing. I happily framed these certificates. In gold. And hung them on my office wall. In my newly acquired office space. Surely, I was up and running. I had my new found knowledge, the desire to help others plus those certificates. Proof as it were; credentials. Things would start happening now. Right?

It took me a while to decide on a career as a Life Coach. It was not a snap decision. As I sat alone in my office, day after day, waiting for the phone to ring, a thought occurred to me. "Christina, you don't know a thing about life!" The more I pondered this thought, the deeper I sank into despair. This was the beginning of my final descent to Zero, though I didn't know it at the time. I had no idea how to make a business grow. I had owned a small dance company in New York, I had been owner, chef, waiter and accountant in my own restaurant. I had failed miserably in both these businesses. Funny, I thought I had already reached Zero!

At some point I said, "Christina, ask for help from anywhere. Stay positive. Figure out what you want, what you really want, what it would take to make you really happy."

Maybe the thing that would make *your* heart sing already exists some-where inside you. Maybe you already have everything it would take to make you happy right here, right now. You just haven't recognized it yet.

This is the very reason for using the concept of Zero in this book.

The universe is change; our life is what our thoughts make it.

– Marcus Aurelius Antoninus

The Meaning of Zero

Zero is a fertile starting place. It is empty yet full. It is the only digit that cannot stand alone. A relationship with other numbers gives it meaning. By itself it is nothing! Ten is merely a one followed by a zero. So understanding the role of zero as marking a particular "place" is essential.

While researching the origins of zero, I came across a marvelous treatise, *Zero in Four Dimensions,* written by Dr. Arsham Hossein, the Wright Distinguished Research Professor in Management Science and Statistics at the University of Baltimore. I actually came across several rather interesting works in addition to his on various aspects of zero that are compelling and well worth the read, should you be so inclined. I've included them in the bibliography at the back of the book.

I'm going to let parts of Hossein's work speak for itself as he writes so well about the subject...

"Zero as a concept, was derived, perhaps from the concept of a void. The concept of void existed in Hindu philosophy and the Buddhist concept of Nirvana, that is: attaining salvation by merging into the void of eternity… in the West, the concept of void and nothingness appeared first in the works of Arthur Schopenhauer during the nineteenth century, although zero as a number had been adapted much earlier. The Greek's emphasis on Geometry kept them from perfecting number notation system. They simply had no use for zero."

Counting is as old as mankind. After we learned to count, numbers were invented and following that, symbolic numerals. The notion of zero was introduced in Europe during the Middle Ages by Leonardo Fibonacci who translated the work of Abu Ja-far Muhammas al Khwarizmi, a Persian scholar. The then-prevalent Roman Numerals did not contain the concept of zero. When European accountants reached zero they pronounced it "empty," an empty hole. This became the present notation of zero, a drawing of a circle, the "empty hole." The actual use of zero as a place holder first appeared as "YY" and was developed by the Babylonians about 1700 BC. Zero wasn't used as a number at that time. The ancient Mayans also used a symbol which looked something like an eye to denote an empty space.

Interestingly enough, in our present day lingo we often avoid the word zero and instead substitute "oh" in its place. An address becomes 243"oh" Main Street instead of verbalizing the word zero. Nowadays, zero also means failure – nothing accomplished. It is also a noun, verb, adverb and an adjective as in "we zeroed in on the cause." Or, in the slang of school age children, a derogatory description of a classmate as in "he's such a zero." A total loser. (I may have my generations mixed up here so please be kind.)

Arsham asks "Is the presence of nothing different from the absence of something or the absence of anything?" Zero is neither positive nor negative but psychologically it is negative. Zero is the something that isn't there.

A few more interesting notes about Zero...

"Nothing will come of nothing" spoke Cordelia, King Lear's daughter when she refused to join in on her sisters scheming against her father. As in life, the entire play unfolds from that very statement. We all know that comedian Jerry Seinfeld built an entire career based upon "a show about nothing" and became a pop icon!

Michael McNeil, author of *The Invention of Nothing*, states that the Arabs or Muslims, generally, didn't invent the so-called present day decimal system. (Arabic numerals). The credit should be given to the Hindus in India decades before Mohammed. The Arabs later picked up the system from the Hindus and eventually passed it along to the far West. "All we really know," says historian D.E. Smith, "is the earliest undoubted occurrence of zero in India is in an inscription of 876."

So what is so magical about Zero?

Zero is the NOW state in the land of having where you mark your own place in time; not worrying about the future or mulling over the past. Zero is the receiving mode. Gregg Braden, in his book, *Secrets of the Lost Mode of Prayer,* says "There is a power that lives in the space "between" that subtle instant when something ends and what follows next hasn't yet begun. From the birth and the death of galaxies, to the beginning and ending of careers and relationships, and even in the simplicity of breathing in and out, creation is the story of beginnings and endings: cycles that start and stop, expand and contract, live and die.

Regardless of the scale, between the "beginning" and the "end" there exists a moment in time when neither one has fully happened. That moment is where magic and miracles come from! In the instant of between, all possibilities exist and none have been chosen. From this place we are given the power to heal our bodies, change our lives, and bring peace to the world. All events originate from this powerful, magical moment."

In this magical moment you give up the need to ask why, when, where and how; all your days will begin at Zero and you will no longer believe you can control all outcomes. Instead you are focused on now. Autopilot is totally disengaged. 100% of your energy is yours to focus on creating the life you want.

I leave this chapter with a quote from Philosopher Joseph Needleman, "Start from Zero, we start from nothing. We start only from our own reason, our own longing, and our own search."

Let us begin the search.

You see things; and you say, 'Why?' But I dream things that never were; and I say, "Why not?

– George Bernard Shaw

Prosperity and The Magic of Zero

S urprise, surprise. We do not make our money, the US Mint makes our money. There is a mint in every country and a treasury which makes its coinage. So, if we don't make money why do we work? Actually we work because we want to or because we think we need to work to be, what we consider, prosperous.

Before we go too far, let's examine two concepts: prosperity and abundance. The two are often confused and they are really totally separate concepts. Abundance, which is a state of mind, is defined as great plenty and it comes from the place where all things come. Some people call it God others call it Spirit. Prosperity, also a state of mind, is generally considered to be a state of success – especially financially. And the Zero place – that's where we all start. It is with us always.

We are taught early on that we must work hard for our money. So, when we work hard, we give ourselves permission to be prosperous, but a job can actually set a ceiling on our abundance. The truth is, if you gave yourself permission to be abundant all the time, you would be regardless of whether you worked or not.

Let's try an exercise. First, imagine that there is an endless store of abundance for you that has nothing to do with your job or your career. If you want, you could use an image that illustrates this. Picture your laundry basket overflowing with money. Next, each night before you go to sleep, use this same picture and focus on filling up the Zero place with a feeling of abundance. Then, imagine that your job is fun and that you do it because you enjoy it. Imagine that your abundance is something separate from your job; it comes from a separate place. You'll be surprised at how this process will start to allow the money to flow – sometimes from totally unexpected sources.

In reality, your money comes from you. You are the source of your own prosperity, not your job. By opening yourself to abundance you allow prosperity. The biggest secret about prosperity is that prosperity is not about money at all. Prosperity is simply a state of mind. And abundance is the state of mind which leads to great plenty. Think of this: How many people do you know who have two or three jobs and are millionaires? None right? On the other hand, haven't you heard of millionaires who, seemingly , don't have to work at all. So the idea that you have to work hard to make a lot of money doesn't really compute, now does it?

Money, whether it is dollars, yen, pesos or seashells is like nothing else in the world. Money can cause a broad spectrum of spontaneous emotions. Money can cause terrible fear, extreme anger and overwhelming joy. Money is tangible, but prosperity is not. Prosperity is an idea, it is of the mind. And, thus, we can cause ourselves to feel the feelings of prosperity; i.e., success, happiness, and peace without ever focusing on the actual dollars and cents.

Money versus the idea of prosperity.

Let us look at the difference between the realities of money versus the idea of prosperity. When you go to the bank and you ask to withdraw money, let's say a few hundred dollars, you are given bills or coins. You can hold these in your hand, you know they are real. But, if everyone decided to withdraw their money at the same time, the bank would not be able to accommodate the demand and would have to close its doors. Why? Because your account is not really filled with "cold hard cash," it's really filled with just the idea of money.

Wealthy people know that the idea of money is what makes the world go round. Wealthy people don't walk around with millions of dollars in their pockets to prove to the world that they are rich. Nor do they have to show a salesperson wads of cash to prove that they can buy a high dollar item. It's all just an idea. In reality, this person may be worth millions, but do they have a roomful of cash or gold and jewels stashed away somewhere? No they don't. Well, not usually. Their wealth is simply represented by numbers followed by a bunch of zeros stored in a computer somewhere. However, unlike most of us, a millionaire is able go to most banks around the world and easily withdraw huge sums of money. But, what truly makes this person wealthy is their knowledge of this ability, not the fact itself.

You can create this same knowledge inside yourself without having a single cent in the bank. Your subconscious mind does not know the difference between the idea of wealth and the reality of wealth. Programming your mind to believe in wealth will cause your subconscious to step up to the plate and create the wealth. The same principle applies if you constantly focus on the lack in your life; your reality will then reflect that which you lack in your life.

The key to prosperity is so simple that you really may not believe it. If you find that you're frequently asking yourself the questions why, how, when or what, then you are not in a receiving mode. You must let go of what you think your life should be. Stop thinking and worrying about what you lack in your life. Stop waking up in the morning with the hard fist of fear in your gut. Remember, like attracts like. Whatever you worry about you attract more of. Our society places so much value on the dollar that we are programmed from a young age to be afraid and worry about whether there is enough money and whether we will run out. Relax, this is an area where you have a choice.

So, how do we change our focus from lack to abundance?

First, petition your higher self. You can say "Please, just help me let go of whatever I need to in order to have a joyful fulfilling life. For that is what I want."

It is important to let go of struggling and needing to struggle. You can ask to uncover the source of your fear and then ask for this source to be healed both in the past and in the present. You can ask to be more at peace in your daily life.

Next, ask yourself how you would like your life to be. Maybe you say to yourself, "Well, I would like to make a lot more money so that I'm not always behind on the bills and I would like to have a bigger house." What would it take for you to have those things? Then maybe you say again, "A lot more money!" Well, what would it take for you to have a lot more money?

Let's contemplate the nature of having more money. The real question is why don't you have enough? Why is it that you *never* seem to have enough? Maybe you are trying the wrong techniques or maybe you're not aware of the forces that are working in your life. Every person goes through difficult times. If you get too caught up in the difficulty then you are not focusing on a way out.

You may be practicing all the abundance techniques you know; things appear to be progressing. Then you are tested. And you find it takes a split second for you to revert to your old patterns of thinking. Maybe you are giving up too easily. You let fear and anger get hold of you and then you lose the momentum that you have created and all that time and hard work becomes irrelevant. I'm sure you have seen many movies where the hero/heroine is running from certain danger. They can feel the hot breath of evil on the back of their neck. Then, instead of kicking into high gear they look back to see how far ahead they are. And what happens? Crash! They trip on a tree root and fall flat on their face in the path of their pursuer! Keep going forward. Resist the need to see how far you have come.

Ok, you've asked for help, you're waiting for instructions. You're digging deep and working on yourself like crazy. Personal changes are occurring daily. You have aligned yourself with the forces of the universe and put yourself in the flow of prosperity...

So, what should you be doing with your life in the meantime?

You, yourself, don't need to be perfect before you do anything. Your life doesn't need to be perfect before you do anything. The truth is the perfecting comes through the doing. So be bold and brave in everything you do. You may already be courageous in many ways. Remember your courage and use the memory of it to spark courage in other areas. Whether you decide to start in the middle or you start at the beginning, don't worry, just start. If you don't, it won't happen. Be honest with yourself but don't take yourself too seriously.

They always say time changes things, but you actually have to change them yourself.

– Andy Warhol

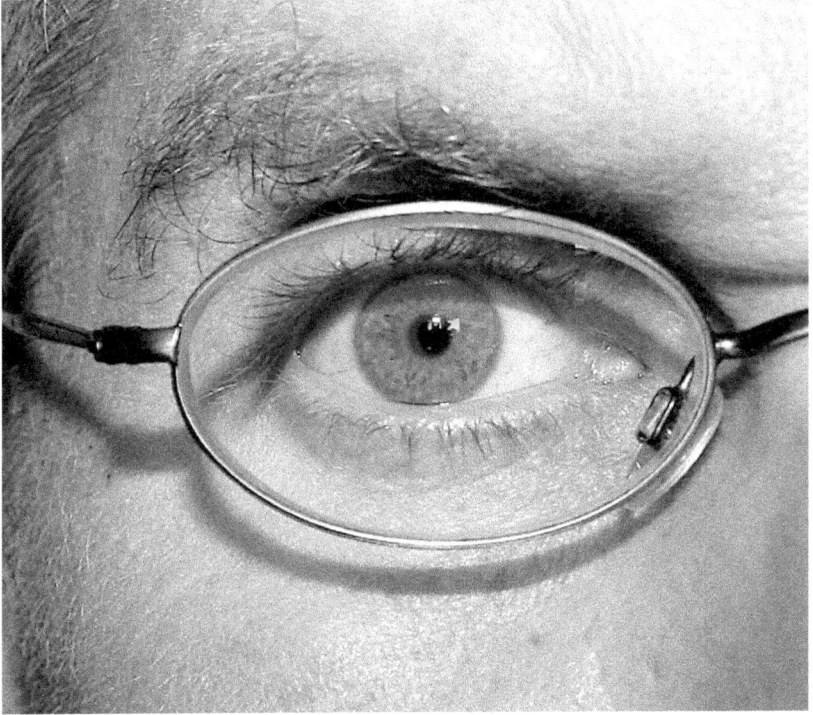

Influencing Your World

I have always thought that if life was exactly the way I wanted it to be I wouldn't need to live it! So I deliberately set out to make things difficult. I always looked for the "feeling bad" part of everything. And, as you can guess, I always found it. I remember one particular dance audition, just before I stepped into the room I had the thought "this feels too easy." Instantly I was anxious and completely forgot the steps. I guess I got what I asked for, it wasn't too easy. In fact it wasn't easy at all.

Here's the thing; life doesn't have to be difficult. We just make it difficult because then we feel as though we are doing something. In fact, it is so easy to get what we want that we don't believe it. The hard part of asking for what you want is trusting and waiting for it to show up. Spiritual teacher, Marianne Williamson, in *The Course in Miracles*, says the Course counsels whatever the problem "Ask to see things differently." What is so hard about that? Just ask! I've tried this, and it really does work. Ask for anything, anything that will make you happy.

The secret to being happy is… to be happy. Oh sure, I can hear you snickering already, and how do I just be happy? Lynn Grabhorn, in her book, *Excuse Me Your Life is Waiting,* asks us to focus on something that makes us feel happy for just 16 seconds a day. You can change your life. Imagine, only 16 seconds! Think of a trip you took, a game well played, a close friend, someone you love.

When I was studying to be a ballet dancer in New York City, the dancers would congregate in the hall and wait to go into class. Because we were all "serious" dancers, we would not be gossiping or gabbing but stretching and practicing. But we were all watching each other out of the corners of our eyes. In class most of the dancers would be concentrating on their moves but I couldn't get beyond the "before class watching." In my mind I was feeling judged and criticized. Why? I was comparing myself to all the other dancers in the world and coming up short. Which means that *I had taken my focus off my goal, i.e., to be the best dancer I could be.* I had put the focus outside myself by comparing myself to all the other girls. I also found myself in constant judgment of other dancers and therefore assumed that they were doing the same of me.

What happens when you lose focus?

Start with your *own* view and move outward from there. Why do we pay undue attention to other people? It is a choice, a choice not to pay attention to ourselves.

It is a choice to look outward instead of inward, where the real work is. What do we gain from not paying attention to ourselves? We get to hold on to an identity which is created by our outside world, or how we think others view us. We see ourselves in other people and yet we fail to see the reality which is that other people are just mirrors, reflecting ourselves back to us. I know people who look in the mirror every day and judge themselves. "You are a failure, you're fat, and you're ugly. You will never get ahead" What if you were to look in the mirror everyday and say "You are beautiful, you are a great success." Truly you would begin to believe these things about yourself. So how does all this negative or positive self-talk relate to your ego? Let's look more closely at the concept of the ego.

Webster's dictionary defines the ego as "the I, or self of any person." If the ego is self than what is self? Is self a part of you that you are born with? Or is it something that you become? I believe that ego is the part of ourselves that is of this world, therefore we can control it. We can make our ego do whatever we want it to do.

I never really made it big as a ballet or a modern dancer, even though I envisioned that I would be a big star some day. Back when I was dancing, I used to be amazed at how gutsy some of those dancers were. What was different about them, or me, for that matter? They never missed the chance to go to an audition. I, on the other hand couldn't wait till I got "cut" so that I could be done with the audition. If you've ever been to an audition, especially one in New York, commonly called "cattle calls," you know how painful they are. Those people that love the audition process will tell you it's just that, a process. To them the process is fun. They don't think about the outcome, they just do it.

To me the process was too nerve-racking. I was overly concerned with how I looked and how everyone viewed my performance. Are you beginning to understand why I didn't have huge success as a dancer? I wouldn't let myself. I was altogether too self-conscious. I never just let go and enjoyed the show! Which brings me back to my point about ego; *The ego is like a shoe on the floor in the middle of a room in the middle of the night. You never know when it's going to trip you up just when you're making your way to someplace important.*

What I have learned all these years later, is that it was never about the end result, it was only about the process; letting go and being pulled into the momentum of the process. The other dancers really loved to dance and they took any opportunity to do so. But I was caught up in my "identity" as a dancer and watched every move that I made from the outside. My *ego* was dictating my life.

This is what I call "being without." When you are focused only on the outside world you are "without" yourself. You are not in touch with your inner knowledge or intuition. You can't possibly make decisions based upon what's best for yourself when you are "being without." Looking back on my ill-fated dance career, I can see that I really was a good dancer but, unfortunately, I was too insecure to ensure long term success. It was my perception of how others viewed me (living "without") that prevented me from getting out of my own way. This perception kept me from acknowledging and more importantly *enjoying* my own talent and success. That is one of the main reasons why, all these years later, I chose to become a Life Coach.

The Magic of Zero at work.

One thing I have always done is to remind my clients that they are in control of their own lives. Here is a little exercise you can do right now. It is a simple way you can observe *The Magic of Zero* at work in your life. Make a list of all the people and things around you that you have some effect on. This is your sphere of influence. Picture yourself standing in the middle of this sphere of influence, radiating energy outward. If you are having a bad day and the energy you send out is angry, imagine that all those people and things in your sphere are pulling in that anger. The people and things that absorbed your negative or anger energy now begin to send that very energy back to you. This is called the **Law of Attraction**. Like attracts like, you create your own universe. Believe it or not, what we perceive as inanimate objects are also capable of responding to your energy too. Keep in mind that trying to *change* anything outside of yourself (your sphere) rarely works, but changing yourself does. You can easily monitor how changing your own state of mind can influence the world outside of you by seeing how others respond to you.

By this, I mean that no one sees life in exactly the same way that you do. You can easily see how the concept of "like attracts like" has played an important role in your perception. Charles Fillmore, founder of Unity School, said that "every person produces a thought atmosphere that has character and power in direct proportion to his ability as a thinker. When you follow narrow ideals your thought atmosphere is correspondingly narrowed but mental breath enlarges and strengthens it in all directions."

Practice consciously changing the energy that you send out. You can do this very simply by smiling. Use smiling as a way to change your environment. When you smile you automatically feel happier. As you do this, you will notice that the people around you change, too. They lighten up and smile back! Interesting, isn't it, how much power you have over your environment. Also notice how, when you really get into feeling good, things around you change. When I smile a lot I notice that the room I'm in begins to look softer, and more inviting. I'm not kidding, this really works. I know that some of you are thinking that this sounds too simplistic, but the real test is when you're feeling really mean and angry. Try this simple little trick and see what happens. Try it. You'll be amazed. Smiling is like a dimmer switch, taking all the negative energy to Zero. I call this *feeling it into being*. In other words, creating the feeling of what you want and focusing on the good feeling of the outcome.

For instance, if a trip to an exotic locale is what you want, how does that dream vacation **feel** when you picture yourself there?

Another way to do this is what Joe Vitale calls "TIISG." Which stands for: Turn it into Something Good. He goes on to say "You have the ability to do this it's a choice. No matter what happens, take a breath and ask "How can I turn this into something good? The question redirects your mind. Instead of looking at the problem, you are now looking for solutions."

This is *The Magic of Zero* at work.

As we express our gratitude, we must never forget that the highest appreciation is not to utter words, but to live by them.

– John F. Kennedy

Gratitude –
Welcome to the Land of Having

O ne day I had an epiphany. *Even though I love to shop, I am not often grateful for the things I buy.* I realized that the minute I have the object of my desire I no longer care about it! Somehow the yearning, the longing for it, is the juicy part; the desire that fuels my days.

I had been coveting this particular pair of shoes. Every day as I passed that shop I gazed longingly at the shoes. Oh, how I wanted those shoes. They were way out of my price range at that time but I was determined to have them. If I had those shoes my life would be complete. I could just imagine them on my feet as I glided gracefully down the street. Friends exclaimed in awe, "Oh, those shoes! Where on earth did you find them?" Then one day I found the very same shoes on the internet for 75% off. Oh, Joy! This was it. The shoes were mine! If I possessed them I would truly, at last, be happy. I wasted no time ordering them. Time slowed as I awaited their arrival. When they didn't arrive promptly as expected, I called the store demanding to know what happened to my shoes. Where are my shoes? What has happened to my shoes? There had been a delay. The shoes had been shipped to the wrong address. I spent considerable time straightening out that confusion, but finally, they were definitely on the way. Oh, yes! My shoes were on the way. Now I could think of nothing but the mailbox. Finally the yellow slip appeared summoning me to the Post Office to collect my package. My shoes had arrived! I was tearing into the wrapping on my way back to the car. I wanted them on my feet right now! And there they were. Just as I had expected, I stared in delight. A perfect fit, a flattering style, a yummy color and such a deal... but suddenly I felt let down, I was not complete. This was not it. My beautiful shoes. Ah well, I slid them off my feet, returned them to their box and threw them over my shoulder into the back seat of the car. I drove home, my mind already focused on surfing the net for my next perfect, fulfilling purchase.

This sad little drama does not play in *my* head alone. Is this a sickness? Millions of Americans are looking for the next best thing. We are in a constant state of yearning and we are not happy. As Judy Levine says in her book, *Not Buying It*, "Possession affords a flicker of warmth which almost inevitably cools. Then we want something else, something different, something better, something less attainable." I wanted to be only in the longing, the "wanting" state. I didn't know how to live in the "having" state. I was boldly ungrateful. My days were defined by finding the next thing, desiring it without reserve, plotting a way to attain this thing, meet this person, or travel to this destination. I was consumed. I would finally attain my goal and be happy. (Sometimes even for a couple of months, sometimes for mere minutes.) Then it's off to the next round of finding, desiring, planning, acquiring. Alas, the "Stuck-ness Monster" rears its ugly head again. *Having is not the same as wanting.*

How to live in the land of having?

What does this "thing" that you "want" do for you? Why doesn't it have the same effect on you once you have it? Welcome to the land of "having." The land of having is indeed the land of *The Magic of Zero*.

Here's something to think about. When you attain this thing, it automatically goes into the "having" world. You, however, are still in the "wanting" world. As long as this is the case you will never truly feel as though you "have" anything. You will be forever wanting and unappreciative. When you live in the "having" world you are living NOW.

The secret to living in the land of having is to desire something without "wanting" it. But, how do you not want something? It's not that you don't want or desire anything; instead you delight in the receiving of it. Living in the land of having allows you to desire without that very desire controlling you. Wanting leads inevitably to yearning and despair which locks you into a tight little cage where you find yourself like the hamster in its wheel, spinning, spinning, spinning. Get off the "gotta have it" treadmill! I know, I can hear you saying "But how? How? It's not just a wave of a magic wand." My response is that I can't honestly give you all the answers or the step by step instructions we so often petition the Universe for. I can however, give you one of the answers. *Be grateful for each precious desire made manifest.* If you were truly, dare I say it, **Unworthy**, the Universe would not allow you to partner in the manifestation of anything you desire, let alone the big stuff.

Insatiable wanting is like a feeding frenzy.

You are on autopilot. Keep your attention on the now. Engage your mind. The devil is in the details but God is most certainly there too. Paying attention requires practice. Frederick and Mary Brussat say in

Spiritual Literacy "All kinds of wonderful and important things are going on right in front of us but we miss most of them because we are not awake. Attention is the intention to live without reservation in the here and now." Take yourself off autopilot and you enter into a whole new world of wonders.

Question life and be prepared to come face-to-face with rationalization. The persuasive little sirens of your ego will paint you pretty little pictures in an attempt to keep you on your treadmill and ruin your self-esteem.

For my part, I had to recognize that I had little or no self-esteem. I was looking outside myself for anything that would make me look or feel good. These things I felt I must have were like band-aids. Every dress, every new pair of shoes, never addressed the problem. And we all know that band-aids need replacing every few days, but buying a new "thing" every day leaves no time for gratitude.

We can't focus on gratitude when we are filled with desire and want. Buddha counseled "The cause of suffering is selfish craving." Wanting is in direct opposition to appreciating what you already have. Interestingly enough, the same issue is as appropriate now as it was in the time of Buddha. Well, that was a long time ago and we are still doing the same thing!

Gratitude is defined as *thankful appreciation for favors received*. Gratitude links you to the Divine which then allows not only the flow of Prosperity but also a sense of well-being. Living in a state of unquenchable wanting creates an undercurrent of hopelessness, a negative state, which blocks the connection with the Divine which, in turn, blocks the path to prosperity and joy.

The Magic of Zero allows you to desire something, create it in your life and then be truly grateful for it each and every day. In the "having world" you feel good. There is a sense of well-being and peace. You are complete. There are no compulsions. You can still feed but now there is no urgency. The whirlwind energy of the frenzy has subsided. Let's face it, compulsion is *exhausting*.

Many years ago I had an artist friend from South America who told me something I have never forgotten. He told me that when he was a child he lived with ten relatives in a one room apartment. Interestingly enough, he said that he never knew he was poor until he grew up because they were all happy to be together and to share everything they had. My friend loved to paint and draw from the time he was very small and he did so with whatever materials he could find. He became known by the people in his neighborhood and upon receiving a scholarship to a famous school of art in New York City, he moved there to continue his studies. He is there still and is now a very well known artist. All he focused on is what he loved to do, paint. He gave no thought to the incredible lack in his life.

My friend would come to mind so often when I was whining about not having enough money for some little thing. I realized that if you focus on misery you just get more misery. What you focus on you get more of. **The Law of Attraction**. If you focus on joy, you get more joy.

Stop the madness!

Sometimes it does feel better just to complain. Indulge then, for, oh, say, one to three days. But, don't forget that while you are wallowing in self-pity you are creating more of what you don't want. Like poison ivy; it seems to feel better when you scratch and then, you want to scratch some more and then, more, and suddenly you can't stop. Keep scratching and you spread the poison fast. To quote Suzanne Powter, *"Stop the madness!"* Learn to manifest through your gratitude.

I used to be able to manifest small amounts of money whenever I needed it. For some reason I did this only when I **needed** the money. Then one day the ability to manifest seemed to go away. I was baffled. For years I couldn't make the money appear when I needed it. I had seemingly exhausted the supply. The more I tried to make the money come to me the worse things got, and the worse things got, the more desperate I became. The more desperate, the more angry I got and … oh no! scratch, scratch, scratch, scratch!

I finally learned about the Law of Attraction. I started, slowly, to think about what made me feel good and I was grateful. The more I did that the better I started to feel. I was putting myself in the feeling of being happy… acting as if. Soon it was no longer acting. And then, amazing! Miracles began to happen.

Every one of us gets through the tough times because somebody is there, standing in the gap to close it for us.

– Oprah Winfrey

Mind the Gap

W hat is happiness? That is the question that is asked millions of times a day in hundreds of languages all over the world, and while I can't answer the question exactly, I can define the *feeling* of happiness very easily. Happiness is peace, it is the absence of worry, and it is contentedness and living in the moment. It is not looking back at past mistakes or looking for future problems. That seems pretty complicated you might say. But, what if I told you attaining happiness and whatever else you want in this world, is as simple as brushing your teeth every day? The truth is that attaining happiness, money, the perfect relationship or anything else does not come from anything you can grab with your hands. It comes from simply remembering one simple notion. Who we are.

The Zero place is really where your so-called "higher self" resides, what Deepak Chopra calls The Gap between your thoughts. Glimpsing this field of quiet, expanded awareness allows us to recognize that our essential self is not the perpetual traffic of thoughts that fill our minds but the silent witness to our thoughts, words and actions. The gap is the link to the field of pure potential. I'd like to clarify here, for those of you who are not familiar with Deepak Chopra's concept of the Gap. He is referring to the gap between thoughts which is a quiet place – the place of Zero. However, there is also another kind of gap, which I refer to in this chapter.

We humans are made up of three parts; the physical body, the emotional body, and the mental body. I feel that while we are in truth, *Spirit*, our bodies are *not* Spirit. Our bodies are three dimensional. The physical is represented by our body parts: feet, hands, eyes, ears, etc. The emotional is represented by our feelings: love, sadness, joy, anger. The mental is represented by our thoughts and our ego. Some people believe that our thoughts create our emotions, others that it is the opposite, that our emotions create our thoughts. I believe it is both.

Experiences often create an immediate emotion on which our thoughts then feed. These thoughts run round and round creating more and more intense emotion. At other times it seems we are not aware of a particular thing until we begin to think about it and then our emotions begin to run wild at what our mind and ego are telling us. Either way, it is the vicious cycle of emotions and thoughts that creates the blocks that cause us to not have the desired outcome. The physical plays an important role in this as well. When we are in physical pain both the mind and the emotions respond with fear.

Fear Factor

Fear is the biggest factor in causing us to not have what we truly want. Fear is the biggest obstacle to who and what we really are. Fear creates conflict, what I call a gap.

When I was visiting in England a few years ago I noticed that at every tube station and at every stop a recorded voice called out "Mind the gap, mind the gap" in reference to the space between the door and the platform. It reminded me that we must "mind the gap" between self and being "without." The place where cobwebs and dust can accumulate. When there is conflict we need to close the gap. Closing the gaps to our happiness and healthiness makes it possible for us to create what we want in our lives. So how do you begin to close these so-called gaps? Author Lynn Grabhorn, who wrote one of my favorite books, *Excuse me your Life is Waiting*, says that in order to create anything you have to *feel* it first. For example if you want to create wealth in your life you have only to feel wealthy. Well, when I read that I thought "Hah, I make $200 a week, how am I supposed to make myself feel wealthy." That was exactly the point. It's a vicious cycle. You don't make enough money, so you don't feel wealthy, you don't feel wealthy so you don't attract ways or think of ways to make more money, you then attract even less money and... Uh oh! scratch, scratch, scratch, scratch, scratch!

This is what I refer to as negative cycling. The Law of Attraction is in action again. Like attracts like. The only way to change the cycle is to change the thought pattern and the only way to change the thought pattern is to change the way you feel. ***Thought plus feeling equals creation.*** When our thoughts and feelings are in line with one another, we can manifest whatever we want. Creating this alignment takes time which may be uncomfortable.

Over the hill is paradise.

Most people have a hard time doing something that they are uncomfortable with for extended periods of time. Changing anything about ourselves takes a long time and it is not usually comfortable, but the good news is that you have the rest of your life to enjoy the new you, so it's worth the discomfort. Change is like walking up a hill with a bag of bricks on your back. Over the hill is paradise. We want to get to paradise by making the changes, but when we get to about the middle of the hill we just get too tired and fall back down onto our backs like an upended turtle and kick and scream that life is unfair and things never seem to change. Sound familiar?

I use a simple, five-minute-per-day, 90-day technique to move you through this process and I ask that you not expect the changes to take place for that amount of time although they can happen much sooner. It is best not to expect complete change before then.

Also, don't get discouraged if you start to feel weird while you are working the process. This is called chemicalization and it is very common. Picture the process as a wave with peaks and troughs. As you progress, the troughs, the places that sink down, become shallower. You will feel more like you are on an even keel without the extreme highs and lows.

Understand that some depression is a normal reaction to change. This knowledge helped me keep pushing through to my 90th day. You will begin to feel a little calmer each day until finally any depression goes away completely. We must push hard to get past the place where we have the tendency to revert back to the old unwanted behaviors. By the way, your diet can also play an important role in the way you feel emotionally and mentally. Drink lots of water and eat lots of leafy green vegetables and this will speed up the process considerably. Really. We are working on the total new you here.

When one door closes, another opens. But we often look so regretfully upon the closed door that we don't see the one that has opened for us.

– Alexander Graham Bell

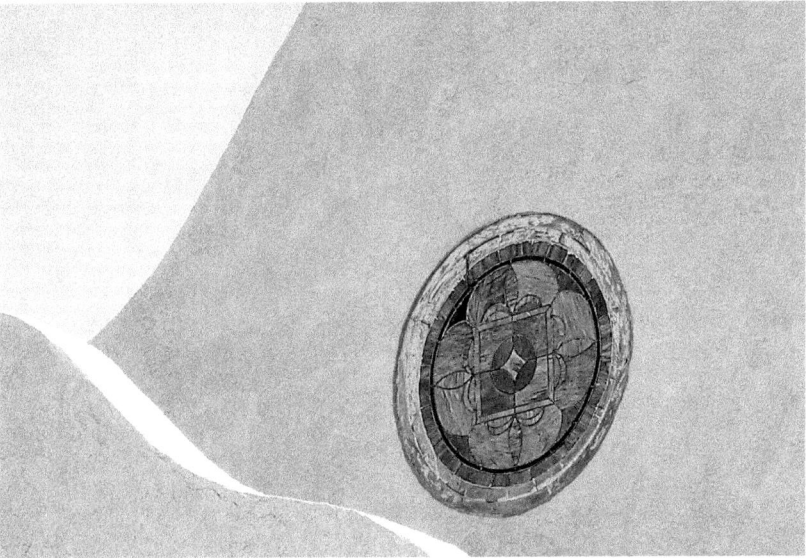

EFT – The Magic of Zero in Action

T he importance of EFT (Emotional Freedom Technique) as a tool for transformation is that it is so effective in getting you out of your own way and allowing you to start everyday at Zero.

EFT is a form of psychological acupressure that uses light tapping instead of needles to stimulate the traditional Chinese acupressure points. The tapping on the designated points on the face and body is combined with verbalizing the identified problem followed by a general affirmation phrase. Combining these ingredients of the EFT technique *balances the energy system* and appears to relieve psychological stress and physiological pain. Restoring the balance of the energy system allows the body and mind to resume their natural healing abilities. EFT is safe, easy to apply and non-invasive.

The above definition of EFT is taken from Carol Look's book *Attracting Abundance with EF*. Her explanation is so concise I really can't improve upon it at all. In this chapter I'm going to give you a few practice statements and affirmations so you can get a feel for how EFT works. I've also included a chart of the eight points on the face and body that you will be using during your practice.

The basic recipe for EFT begins with creating a **Setup Statement**. This statement is repeated three times. It is followed by two rounds of tapping on the eight EFT points. The first time you tap on the eight points you focus on your problem while repeating a **negative reminder** phrase out loud. You repeat the phrase while tapping on each one of the points. The second round of tapping on the eight points **focuses on the solution**. Create phrases that focus on possible positive outcomes. This phrase is also repeated out loud while tapping on the EFT points. The positive phrase can be different for each of the eight points or you can use just the one statement.

Focus on the underlying issue.

Before you begin, focus on the problem state. For example: I have low self-esteem. On a scale of one to ten, with ten being the most intense, how would you rate the feelings associated with this concern? Make note of this number. If you really can't assign a number just make a note of how you feel. Now you are ready to create your setup statement. This statement focuses on the underlying issue of the problem state.

Here are the points you will be tapping:

Top of head

Inside point of eyebrow

Side of eye

Under eye

Under nose

Chin, under bottom lip

Collarbone

Under arm

The following diagram shows the exact spots to tap for each point.

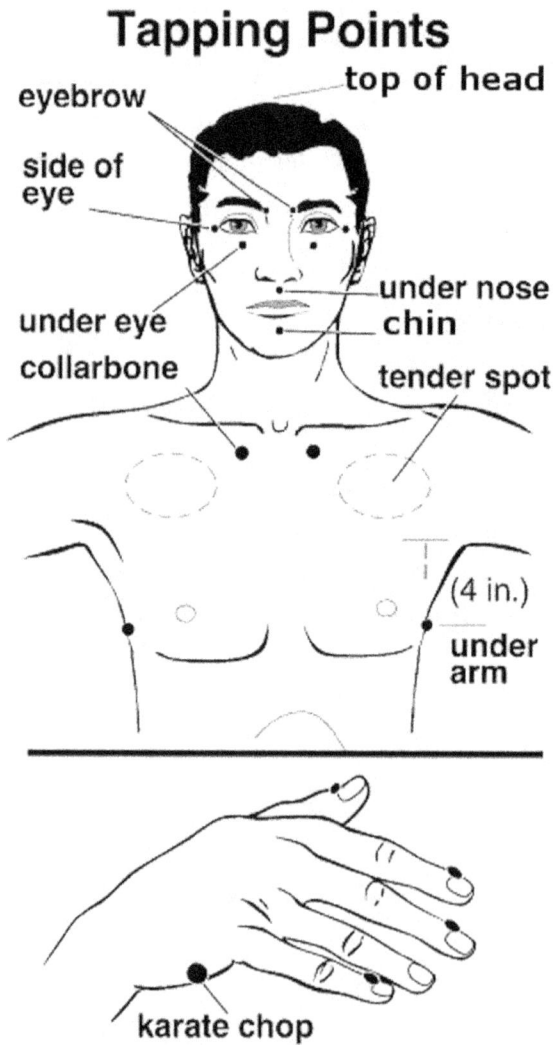

Tapping Points

eyebrow — top of head

side of eye

under eye — under nose

collarbone — chin

tender spot

(4 in.)

under arm

karate chop

Courtesy of Gloria Arenson, author of *Five Simple Steps to Emotional Healing*

Let's begin a sample round.

The Setup Statement

I cannot say enough about the setup statement. This is not only the heart of EFT but also the key to success with EFT.

I always ask a lot of questions before I do my initial statements because I want to make sure I'm on the right track. Remember the setup statement really speaks to the heart of the issue. Some people ask me why the initial setup statements are posed in the negative. EFT works like acupuncture for pain. With acupuncture you are getting treated for pain with needles in the same way you treat your emotional pain with EFT by stating the painful state as you tap on the meridians. This pushing the pain out, so to speak, is the most important part. After you do that, you then go about installing a positive state. At this point your setup statement will reflect a positive outcome, projecting the outcome exactly the way you want it to be. Using all four fingertips of one hand, tap the karate chop point on the side of the other hand continuously while repeating the setup statement. *Repeat the statement three times while tapping*:

"Even though I have this conflict about my self-esteem, I still deeply and completely love and appreciate myself."

Negative Phrase

Begin the first round of tapping on the eight points on the top of your head. Tap at least seven to ten times on each of the eight points while repeating: (Say this phrase just once for each point.)

"This conflict about my self esteem"

Positive Outcome Phrase

This round is reinforcement indicating the desired positive outcome. Tap each point seven to ten times. The positive phrase can be different for each point. Begin with the top of the head repeating each phrase just once at each point.

Top of head: "It feels great to resolve this conflict"

Eyebrow: "I am now releasing this conflict"

Side of eye: "I choose to be free of this conflict"

Under eye: "It feels so good to be free of this conflict"

Under nose: "I appreciate knowing I can change"

Chin: "I choose to resolve this conflict now"

Collarbone: "I choose to feel confident about myself"

Under arm: "I love feeling good about myself"

After you finish these rounds take another assessment of the feelings associated with the problem state. Is the feeling less intense? Where is it on the scale of one to ten? The objective is to tap yourself all the way down to Zero. If you have tapped several rounds and the intensity doesn't appear to be lessening it may be time to create a new setup statement. Repeat the EFT process with your new statement. Make note of the thoughts that arise while you are tapping. It is possible that the issue you are considering as the problem state may not be the issue at all or at least not the primary issue. You can create statements from the thoughts that arise in your mind and tap on these. For instance, about now you may be thinking, "Gee, I really hate this tapping. How can this be doing me any good?" Then you would tap on: *"Even though this stupid tapping doesn't seem to be doing me any good, I still deeply and completely love and appreciate myself"* or *"Even though I don't believe in this tapping thing I still totally and completely accept myself anyway."* Get the picture?

Often, once you have tapped the initial issue down to Zero, you find there are other related issues. It's like peeling an onion. You are trying to get to the core of your own belief systems by peeling back the layers (and hopefully, without too many tears!).

Zero is the only way to be fully functional in manifesting your desires. Again, I suggest two five-minute sessions of EFT every day in order to incorporate the benefits of *The Magic of Zero* into your life.

I have been through some terrible things in my life, some of which actually happened.

– Mark Twain

50 Ways to The Magic of Zero
(well, really only 10)

T hese are ten principles I discovered that changed my life and my ability to manifest whatever I want.

Breathe...

Breathing is the most important thing our body does. It is our life force. Breathing exercises connect us to spirit and open us to our highest good. As Dennis Lewis says in *Free your Breath, Free Your Life*, "Our mostly constricted breathing undermines our physical, emotional, and spiritual well-being. This deprives us without us even knowing it, of one of the greatest joys of living on earth; the expansive sensation of free, easy, boundless breath that engages the whole of ourselves and connects us with all of life."

You can begin with the simplest breathing exercise. Place a hand on your heart and another on your abdomen. Breathe. If the hand on your chest remains almost still and the hand on your stomach moves in and out as you inhale and exhale then you are breathing correctly. Movement of the upper chest only upon inhaling is considered a shallow or incomplete breath. Many of us were taught to stand up straight and hold our stomach in as part of proper posture. Often times the stomach muscles are pulled in merely for appearance sake. This shallow breathing, so often practiced today in our stress filled lives, cannot support us on our path to self-transformation.

Rid yourself of self-deprecating, negative thought patterns...

These are the very thought patterns that create self-defeating situations in your life. When you say negative things about yourself, train yourself to use the delete button. Say "delete" every time you put yourself down. This takes practice and perseverance but soon you will find that you are out of the habit. Ridding yourself of the habit (off autopilot) of putting yourself down is the first and most important step in *The Magic of Zero*. The Zero space is where you wipe everything clean and begin again. Everything I teach in this book is toward that end. Gift yourself with a copy of Dr. Masaru Emoto's incredible book, *Messages From Water*, about the effect of emotions on water. Refer to it daily. Our emotions imprint our cells. Both praise *and* condemnation alter our chemistry on a cellular level.

Here is an easy exercise to imprint "feel good" thoughts. Think of the last time you felt really great about doing something. Focus very hard on the way you felt as you were doing that thing (the good feelings). Now, when you are at the height of feeling good, press the thumb and forefinger of your right or left hand together and hold it there for 20 seconds while you continue having the memory of feeling good. That's called anchoring. You can anchor a good feeling anywhere on your body. Instead of using thumb and forefinger, try pressing a spot on your collarbone. The important part is not where you anchor but that you use your anchor whenever you feel bad. Your body is what holds the memory of feeling, so that when something important happens, the memory of the event is stored somewhere in the body. Anchor a good feeling somewhere where you can find it. Then, when you feel bad, you can press on your anchor point and switch the feeling – a simple technique that really works. You can find more information about anchoring on the internet by searching on NLP.

Stop criticism and judgment of others...

This is difficult. You may struggle with it as I still do. Accept and own your dark side. This is quite often a case of "autopilot." You are in the habit so you no longer even hear yourself. We inflict pain on others by neglecting, gossiping, criticizing, judging, and indifference. We all do this in some small way more than we care to admit. I find that when I'm judging someone just remembering the last time I did the same dumb thing usually stops me. Most likely, someone judged me in a similar fashion for whatever it was, no matter how unimportant. People are complainers. We pick apart co-workers, friends, or the stars of the latest film we have seen. We say, "My, she's not aging well!" We fill our heads with endless chatter about all the things that bother us in the world. Most of it is truly insignificant. Sometimes we do it to make ourselves feel better. Don't confuse this with "venting." There are often legitimate complaints. They can be aired but please, move on quickly.

Honor your own boundaries...

Boundaries emerge from a belief that what we like and dislike as well as what we want and need, is important. If you don't create and respect your own boundaries, no one else will and you'll feel taken advantage of. Setting your own boundaries means that you have the right to say "No" to things that you don't feel are right for you. When you discover the need to set a limit with someone, state your feelings clearly, and preferably without anger, by using as few words as possible. You will be tested. Some people will be hurt by your seeming "inconsideration for their feelings." They may be disappointed and, indeed, angry with you when you enforce your boundaries. Institute a "three strikes and you're out policy"; the number of "strikes" or times people can infringe on your boundaries and get away with it. You have the right to stand up for yourself!

Pay attention...

Pay attention whenever you do something. This may seem obvious to some but I know a lot of people (myself included) who do things unconsciously. It's the "Autopilot" yet again. This can wreak havoc on your day, causing you to misplace things, miss exits on the highway and forget things such as important appointments, etc. We spend too much time worrying about the future and agonizing over the past.

Quite often less than 50% of our Life Energy is present at any given time to tend to what is happening today. We may have 20% at work, another 5% attached to that callous remark made many years ago by someone important to us and yet another 15% projected into future scenarios that will probably never occur. Grounding yourself in the present is a matter of practice. Living in the moment means immersing yourself fully in every experience, be it good or bad. As you learn to embrace the present you will come to realize that a joyful life is a compilation of its moments.

Just do it ...

Take action. Whenever you think of something that you really want to do, take action immediately, because if you don't you will talk yourself right out of it. Think of all the things you might have done had you not missed the moment by thinking too much about it. Count how many times in your life you have said "I wish I had done that." I'm not suggesting you run off willy-nilly into whatever calls to you at the moment. There are obvious considerations for health and safety. Exercise caution but do not spend days running the various scenarios and their myriad possible outcomes through your head or you will be frozen in place. Attraction tells us this: Anything you want in life, anything, requires you to take passionate risks. That means deciding what you want and just doing it without taking to much time to ponder the "what ifs." The "what ifs" are deadly to our dreams.

Push the envelope...

Step outside the box whenever possible. What makes certain people succeed while others do not? It is their ability to push the envelope and to think outside the box. I know this phrase is so over-used but it is still appropriate. Pushing the envelope means going beyond what you think is possible for yourself. If you want to do something big but you are afraid to do it because of reasons like "I'll probably fail," "I could be embarrassed," "I might get rejected" or one of the worst "but, we've always done it this way," then simply push yourself to do something. If it's what you want to do and you find you are already talking yourself out of it, do it anyway.

The mind likes to play games with us, or I should say the ego likes to play games with us. I found the best thing for outwitting the ego is to do something that you don't want to do. Yes, that's right, do something that isn't comfortable. Step outside your comfort zone. Give a speech in front of a small group. This is really a stumbling block for most people. However, public speaking is such a tremendous boost for your self-confidence. You will say to yourself "Hey, I just spoke in front of a bunch of people. I can do anything now!"

Other ways to challenge yourself might be to go to the movies alone. Some people absolutely refuse to do this thinking that being by yourself makes you appear somehow inadequate in the eyes of others. Focus on yourself. You don't know what others are thinking. Sign up for creative writing or oil painting classes. Take a new route home from work. There are many, many things you can do to expand your life. By the way, changing your routines also keeps your mind active and young. You are learning something new no matter how trivial it seems to you. New neurological pathways are being created every time you step out of the box. If you stay in your comfort zone all the time you will never be able to experience anything else.

Be true to your emotions...

Sensing what your emotions have to tell you is the best way to create what you want in your life. Feeling is a conscious perception of emotion. One can't have a thought without a feeling or a feeling without a thought. Emotions are what makes life worth living. They are energy in motion. Emotions are one of our avenues to self-knowledge and may also be the cause of many of our failures of self-knowledge.

Emotions can tell us whether or not we are ready for what we think we want. For example, let's say you want a different job with all of your heart. (You think.) But, your spouse is worried because you have a great benefits package and you can't afford to lose that. Your parents want you to bring the family to visit on your next hard won three-week vacation and you don't want to lose that. Your boss is counting on you to land that account he's been courting for the last year and you don't want to let him down. What emotion is all this creating? Fear. Fear is the biggest emotional block of all. Others may be guilt, anger, defensiveness, helplessness. Any of these fears can stand in the way of getting what we want. These fears not only block productive dialog with others but also with ourselves. Becoming more conscious of our feelings and our emotions is part of the healing process, leading us to discover the power of choice. Think of it this way: thoughts-mind, emotions-heart, feelings-body.

Laugh a lot...

We all love someone who can make us laugh. Share your sense of humor, not only will you feel better but you will find you'll have more friends. Laughter releases endorphins which suppress pain and plain old "makes ya feel good." It boosts our immune system and, as recently discovered, plays a role in healing. Laughter integrates both sides of our brain.

"Angels fly because they take themselves lightly."
– G. K. Chesteron

A sense of humor will help you rise to any challenge, handle the unexpected with ease, and come out of any difficulty with a smile. Humor isn't just about telling jokes. Humor is the way we view the world. We can be honest about life without taking it quite so seriously. We can laugh at ourselves, at our mistakes and pain. Louis Kronenberger explains: "Humor simultaneously wounds and heals, indicts and pardons, diminishes and enlarges; it constitutes inner growth at the expense of outer gain, and those who possess and honestly practice it make themselves more through a willingness to make themselves less." The most wasted day is a day in which we have not laughed.

Be grateful for what you have...

We have so much to be thankful for. I can't say this enough. Often, instead of rejoicing in what we have, we want something more, better, or different. We take things for granted and feel entitled. We can't be grateful because we are making comparisons and imagining ourselves coming up short. We covet other possibilities. When it's our ego that is dissatisfied, then we are ungrateful. A practice of Gratitude doesn't require belief in supernatural things, but rather an attention to

> Gratitude acknowledges our receiving of abundance, and, in and of itself becomes an act of giving back to the Universe. Abundance then becomes a natural by-product of gratitude. How is that possible? How does it suddenly appear? Quite simply... it was always there! We just had not been able to see it.
>
> – *Arasini Foundation*

reality as it is. Every day we are engaged in a miracle which we don't even recognize; walking on this earth. Begin by saying "thank you" for both the joyous and the challenging experiences, for people, animals, art, memories. For changing seasons, for the smell of lilacs in the spring and wood smoke in the fall.

You can begin your practice of gratitude by creating a symbolic gratitude ritual or prayer. You can make an altar of things you like, a piece of art, a place to light incense, a candle. My altar has a statue of Skeet (the original Sun Goddess) and two spheres of alabaster, a light and an incense burner. Choose what pleases you. If an altar does not suit you then maybe a prayer or quiet time spent in a favorite spot, either outdoors or in your favorite comfy chair. There is no wrong choice.

I start each day thanking the sun for light and warmth. I thank my higher self for all the gifts of life and I ask for protection for myself and all my loved ones. Then I ask for what I want; prosperity, clients, health, etc., always remembering to add: Thank you, thank you, thank you, for my _____ I am so very, very, very, grateful. Be specific.

Your work is to discover your world and then with all your heart give yourself to it."

– The Buddha

Tools For Transformation
Exercises to Bring The Magic of Zero into Your Life

The Magic of Zero & Getting Slim

Here is my tried and true method for getting slim. First of all I never say that I want to LOSE weight. The word LOSE makes our inner child very uncomfortable because, really, when you lose something you tend to want it back again. This causes a degree of resistance that is very hard to move through.

So, start by telling yourself that you are going to RELEASE the weight or that you are going to become X amount of pounds lighter, or anything other than LOSE weight! Do not tell yourself that you need to go on a DIET; the word contains within it the word DIE and this makes your inner child and your subconscious really, really uncomfortable! The truth is that if you will just allow this process to work for thirty to ninety days, you will automatically start eating healthy foods and stop craving unhealthy foods. Be patient! Find a way of eating that is healthy and feels comfortable, a way that fits easily into your lifestyle. Use the processes below to rewire your brain so that you can train yourself to eat this way.

When you wake up in the morning, even before you get out of bed, *be grateful for your body*. If you hate your body how do you expect it to do what you want it to do? Picture your body the way you want it to be and say: "*Body I love you and thank you for my good health and my healthy weight of XXX lbs.*"

Find a picture of a person whose body you just love. Then, find a picture of yourself that you like. Cut your head out of the picture and tape it on to the other body that you like. (Make sure your head will fit on the other picture so that it looks believable to you.) Do not just use a picture of yourself when you were thin as this sets up a series of other belief systems that will cause you to fail (i.e. "I was so much younger then" or "I was so sad then" etc.) And remember failure is not an option! Write underneath this new photo, in big letters "Your name... your weight is... (your target weight). (Example: Ann, your weight is 125 lbs.) Put this next to your computer or next to your bathroom mirror. It is imperative that you look at it every day for 30 to 90 days!

Please do not weigh yourself for the first 30 days. You are doing something radically different and weighing yourself may sabotage the process.

Next, imagine four knobs or slide buttons (like dimmers for lights) in front of you. These represent: Sugar, Fat, Carbs and Metabolism. After each meal take your hand and physically move the first three knobs to "0." As you do this feel your body releasing the urge to "hold on" to these things. Move the metabolism knob to HIGH. Feel your body's metabolism start to go into high gear.

If you feel that your weight is due to hormonal issues, add a knob for hormones and move it to the middle position marked "balance."

This next step I am going to teach you is a very radical process.

Here's how it works:

Imagine a picture of yourself in front of your face as you are now. Make this picture very real by adding the feelings you have about your current body weight. Then make the picture black and white and make it the size of a postage stamp. Now, move it down to your left.

Imagine a picture of yourself at the weight you want to be (you can use the new photo that you created in the last process). Make this picture very vivid in your mind. (If you are not a visual person just feel the energy of being the weight that you want to be.) Add feelings to the picture and sounds and smells if you want; make it rich. Now, make this picture postage stamp size and put the color picture of yourself down to the right. Bring up the black and white picture of yourself as you are now and make it large again. Again, focus on the feeling of it. Now, quickly move the color picture up to take its place while you clap you hands loudly. Make the color picture larger than life! Infuse it with feelings of happiness and music or smells or tastes of healthy foods. This creates a hologram of **how you want to be**. Do this three or four times until you can no longer find the black and white picture of yourself in your mind.

Some people find it easier to have a friend take them through this process and this works just as well (sometimes even better). I also highly recommend having a weight reduction partner for moral support.

Finally, and most importantly: **Use EFT on your weight issues for three to five minutes every day**.

Go to the EFT Chapter and familiarize yourself with the process.

Here are just some of the hundreds of statements that you can use:

"Even though I hate my body the way it is right now, I still totally and completely love and accept it anyway."

"Even though it feels as if I will never get to my target weight of XXX pounds, I still totally and completely love and accept my body anyway."

Here's a great setup statement from Rebecca Marina, EFT Master:

"Even though I crave _____ , I ask the opiate receptors in my brain to be dulled to _____ now." Tap all the way down to zero saying "Opiate receptors in my brain are dulled to _____ now." Do this whenever you have a craving for an unhealthy food. Then tap on "I ask my body's intelligence to give pleasure from eating healthy foods that support my weight of XXX."

You can also visit my website at www.themagicofzero.com for more statements and other EFT tools you can use.

You can compliment your EFT practice with one of my favorite techniques – the "**Magic Mirror.**" I have described this technique in detail in the Abundance chapter. See yourself at your ideal weight in stylish new clothes. Your subconscious mind will work to create the new you that you envision in the mirror.

One more thought. Find a few **easy** physical exercises (and I mean easy) that you can do for three to five minutes everyday. Start small – you can build up to more later. The idea is to ease yourself into enjoying these exercises by making them fun and easy to do. You don't need to exert yourself to benefit from exercise! If you like to walk, take a short or long walk whenever you can. Sing a song like "I feel pretty" or "I'm too sexy for my _____ " while you exercise or walk.

Do EFT on "Even though I am not motivated to exercise, I still totally and completely love my body anyway."

Have fun changing your body weight. Laugh and play and enjoy every bite of food that you eat. Thank your food and be grateful to it for giving you nourishment and enjoyment and your food will thank you by making you healthy!

The Magic of Zero and Creating Abundance

The Magic of Zero also works well for prosperity and abundance issues.

Here's how it works:

Begin by picking a time in the day when you have about five to ten minutes and do three or four of the following exercises. You can switch the exercises around so that you don't get bored or you can stay with the same ones if you like routine. Again, stick with this for 90 days. You will most likely see changes before that but don't get discouraged if you don't. Changing your "money madness" can take time. After all it has probably been with you for many years.

Breaking Through the Barriers

This is a great exercise for those people who feel they have a "ceiling" on their income. You can visualize or just feel this exercise.

Sit in a quiet place and imagine yourself at the start of a foot race. Imagine (feel or see) yourself crouched down waiting for the starting shot.

Hear the shot and picture yourself taking off running. Feel your foot push against the ground to urge you forward. Imagine a huge canvas with your current income written on it in large numbers. The canvas is directly in your path. Burst through the canvas with your arms raised as if you are winning the race. Feel the exhilaration as if you have won a race. See a new canvas in front of you with a higher amount on it. Run through this one feeling the same exhilaration. Imagine a crowd cheering you on as you crash through these income barriers. Know that there are no longer limits on your income. Repeat this process going for higher and higher amounts until you reach your target income. As you break though the final income barrier see yourself jumping for joy! The crowd goes wild!!!

The Magical Zeros

Take your bank statement and look at it. Notice how the total makes you feel. Now white out all the numbers except the first digit. Then take a black pen and add a comma and six zeros and look at it again. How do you feel now? Put this up on your refrigerator and look at it every day!

A Star In My Throat

This exercise can be done anywhere, any time and takes about 45 seconds:

Imagine (see or feel) a bright light (like a star or a bright car headlight) about six inches above your head. Now bring the star out in front of you and down to about two inches above your navel. Bring the star inside your body just at that point and imagine it getting brighter.

Bring the star up into your solar plexus and imagine it getting brighter. Now bring it up to your heart area and make it brighter. As you bring the star up to your throat area place it in the hollow of your throat and this time make it extremely bright, make it excessively bright or blindingly bright! Let it stay there for about 20 seconds. This area is the abundance center. Now bring the star up to your third eye for a few seconds and then exit out the top of your head. Repeat as often as you like. I manifested $10,000 once just a short time after I did this exercise!

As always I recommend these expressions of gratitude:

"Thank you, thank you, thank you for my income of _____ . I'm so very, very grateful."

"Thank you, thank you, thank you for my windfall of _____ . I'm so very, very grateful."

"Thank you _____ for my many clients" or "my perfect job" or "my successful business" or "my pay raise of _____ " and so on and so on.

Remember that you will really feel the gratitude welling up inside you if you say the words "I'm so very, very grateful." Try it. Gratitude works every time.

The Magic Mirror

Sit in a quiet place and close your eyes. Imagine a beautiful staircase in front of you. There are ten stairs. Picture the details, polished wood, cement, or maybe an oriental stair runner. Walk down the stairs while you count backwards from one to ten relaxing more with each step down.

At the bottom of the stairs is a room with doors leading to other rooms. Each door has a title over it; Great Wealth, Perfect Weight, etc. Go to the door with the title you want to create for yourself. Open the door and enter the room. The room is comfortable and filled with all the items that make up the thing that you want for yourself. It feels so good to be in this space.

At the back of the room you notice a closet. The closet is filled with all the things you will wear when you become the way you want to be. Take out an article of clothing that represents the "New" you. Put on the clothing and walk over to the full length mirror on the wall next to the closet. This is a magic mirror. Do you see yourself? If not, find a picture of yourself in your mind or think of a picture of a person who represents what you want to be. Stick that picture on the mirror.

Now notice the series of dials on the bottom of the mirror. Use these dials to make yourself look exactly the way you want to look. Adjust the "you" in the mirror until it fits your idea of how you want to be. Turn around and step backwards into the mirror. *Feel* the way it feels to be the new you.

Notice there is a button marked "Enter" on the mirror. See yourself looking, acting and feeling like the new you then press the button. Your subconscious mind will search, just like a computer, to create this new way of being for you. When you feel as though you have completely embodied your new being, step out of the mirror, and *be* your new self. Turn to face the mirror one last time and hit the "Enter" button again. Leave the room and return to the outer room. Take the escalator you have just noticed, riding up while counting from one to five. On five open your eyes and smile!

The Power of Intention

I have one last exercise to tell you about that will assist you in the creation of abundance. Using the power of intention is an easy way to manifest anything you desire. State your intention. That is, decide what you want. You may want to make it something small to begin with until you get the hang of it. A small intention may be to have a parking space in front of the movie theatre. "I intend that I find a parking space that is mine right in front of the theatre." Say it as if the space is already there, with feeling. The feeling is what makes it happen. Put your intention out there and then forget about it. When your intention materializes you will be amazed.

In Esther Hicks book, *Ask and it is Given*, there is a part she calls **Segment Intending**. A segment can be as small as two minutes. The idea is that your day is broken into more manageable segments. This is often an easier concept to grasp than attempting to script an entire day without adequate practice. Go through each segment of your day intending that it be just the way you want it to be. When I first read this I used it for all sorts of things and had a lot of fun with it. I used this technique to manifest all green traffic lights from my home to my office. And so that there would be no line at the bank, I'd say "I intend that there is no line at the bank today." And, voila! I walk right up to the teller.

Many years ago, before I even knew about the power of intending I had the most miraculous experience. I had been wanting a new car but I couldn't afford one. I earned very little income, and my credit was far from exemplary. I had placed a picture of a little red car up on my refrigerator and wrote the words "my car" under it. Gradually the picture became covered up with other miscellaneous scraps of paper. One day, a few months later, my car just died. I didn't know what I was going to do. Thinking my situation hopeless, I resigned myself to taking the bus. The next day while bemoaning my bad luck to a friend at her nail salon a woman sitting next to me said "I can get you a car." "Right" I said. "I don't even have a real job." "No really" she said "I'm the head of finance of Castle Chrysler." She asked if she could say that I worked at the salon. My friend happily agreed and I gave the woman my information. This conversation was on a Friday.

Over the weekend I decided I would buy a friend's old clunker (figuring I'd never hear from this woman again). So, Monday morning as I was heading out to sign the papers on my friends car the phone rang. "Hi Christina, I have your car ready for you, come pick it up whenever you want." Well, you can imagine my surprise! I said "What? I can't afford a new car with my credit. The interest alone would kill me!" She rattled off the price, the interest, the terms and payments which, surprisingly, I could totally afford. And, this car was loaded! I'm thinking, where's the catch? No catch. So I went down to the dealership, signed the papers and drove out of the lot 45 minutes later. That has got to be the fastest anyone has ever bought a new car. I drove my new red car for many years without a single problem.

...That's magic!

Final Thoughts

Well, there you have it. How to live life in the land of the having. My hope is that you will use this as a daily guide for permanent positive change so that you don't, as I did for so many years, get lost at the bottom searching for the door to the top.

Be kind to yourself, learn to love yourself, and above all be patient while you apply these tools for the 90 days necessary to change your life.

Remember to be conscious every day, be present every day. Life is a gift. Notice it. Look around you and see what is out there. Then look inside and see what is in there.

And, as the Vulcans say, "Live long and prosper!"

Bibliography

Callings: Finding and Following an Authentic Life, Gregg Levoy, (Harmony 1997)

Excuse Me Your Life is Waiting, Lynne Grabhorn, (Hampton Roads Publishing Co. 2003)

Zero in Four Dimensions: Historical, Psychological, Cultural, and Logical Perspectives, Dr. Arsham Hossein, (The Pantaneto Forum 2002)

Attracting Abundance With EFT, Carol Look LCSW, DCH, (Author House 2005)

Spiritual Literacy: Reading the Sacred in Everyday Life, Frederic and Mary Ann Brussat, (Scribner 1996)

Anatomy of the Spirit, Caroline Myss, Ph.D., (Three Rivers Press 1996)

Not Buying It: My Year Without Shopping, Judith Levine, (Free Press 2006)

The Attractor Factor, Joe Vitale, (John Wiley & Sons 2005)

Secrets of the Lost Mode of Prayer, Greg Braden, (Hay House 2006)

Ask and It Is Given: Learning to Manifest Your Desires, Esther & Jerry Hicks, (Hay House 2004)

Recommended Reading
(not included in Bibliography)

Secrets of the Millionaire Mind, T. Harv Eker, (Collins 2005)

The 40 Day Prosperity Plan, John Randolph Price, (Hay House 2004)

The Abundance Book, John Randolph Price, (Hay House 1996)

Your Faith is Your Fortune, Neville, (DeVorss & Co 1985)

The Law & the Promise, Neville, (DeVorss & Co 1984)

Dynamic Laws of Prosperity, Catherine Ponder, (DeVorss & Co 1985)

How to be Wildly Wealthy FAST, Sandy Forster, (Universal Prosperity, 2nd edition, 2004)

The Writings of Florence Scovel-Shinn, (DeVorss & Co. 1988)

Life is Short – Wear Your Party Pants, Loretta LaRoche, (Hay House 2004)

The Invisible Path to Success: Seven Steps to Understanding and Managing the Unseen Forces Shaping Your Life, Robert Scheinfeld, (Hampton Roads Publishing Co. 2003)

The Nothing That Is, Robert Kaplin, (Oxford University Press 1999)

About the Author

Christina Florence is an internationally known Life and Prosperity Coach. Born and raised in Albuquerque, New Mexico, she received her BA from UNM after which she moved to New York City in 1980 to continue her education. There, she discovered her abilities as a teacher and businesswoman. Since then her skills have been complemented by an extensive commitment to self-improvement through modalities such as EFT, hypnosis and NLP. This self-improvement led her to pursue studies in all of these areas, which subsequently created a profound desire in her to help others.

Christina has varied interests in both her business and personal life. Her Renaissance-woman style has led her to combine her accomplishments in the business world, including the operation of a successful restaurant in Albuquerque's historic Old Town, which became a haven for patrons seeking good food and stimulating conversation in a warm and inviting atmosphere. She is a gourmet chef, former host of the talk show, OM Talk, and is currently writing a novel. She maintains a private practice and leads Prosperity seminars for clients and local civic organizations.

Christina's mission is to ensure her sessions provide the necessary support, encouragement and understanding that's needed to effect changes and bring balance to her clients' professional and personal lives. She is particularly focused on the empowerment of battered women and young people.

She lives with her husband, Walter, and their two dogs in Corrales, New Mexico.

FOR MORE INFORMATION, see The Magic of Zero website.
Website: **www.themagicofzero.com**
Email: **info@themagicofzero.com**

www.ingramcontent.com/pod-product-compliance
Lightning Source LLC
LaVergne TN
LVHW021522080426
835509LV00018B/2621